$7.16
E-P
1/80

Bigfoot: Man, Monster, or Myth?

by
Carrie Carmichael

A

Book

From

RAINTREE CHILDRENS BOOKS
Milwaukee • Toronto • Melbourne • London

Library of Congress Number: 77-21317

Art and Photo Credits

Cover illustration by Lynn Sweat.

Photos on pages 7, 22, 33, and 36, The Bigfoot Information Center and Exhibition.
Illustrations on pages 9, 11, 14, 23, 27, 32, and 42, Nilda Scherer.
Photos on pages 19 and 30, Peter Byrne, The Bigfoot Information Center and Exhibition.
Photos on pages 20, 38, and 44, Wide World Photos.
Photo on page 46, George B. Schaller/Bruce Coleman, Inc.
All photo research for this book was provided by Sherry Olan.
Every effort has been made to trace the ownership of all copyrighted material in this book and to obtain permission for its use.

Library of Congress Cataloging in Publication Data

Carmichael, Carrie.

Bigfoot: man, monster, or myth?
SUMMARY: An inquiry into the existence of the purportedly half-human, half-animal creatures said to have roamed the northwestern states and British Columbia for hundreds of years.
1. Sasquatch—Juvenile literature.
[1. Sasquatch] I. Title.
QL89.2.S2C37   001.9'44   77-21317
ISBN 0-8172-1052-0 lib. bdg.

Manufactured in the United States of America
ISBN 0-8172-1052-0

Contents

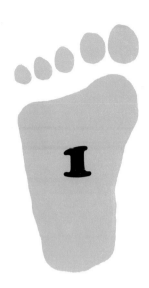

The Kidnapping of Albert Ostman

It was the summer of 1924. Summer is the time of the year when all the world seems to be off on a holiday. Albert Ostman decided that he, too, would take a holiday trip. Ostman, a 34-year-old construction worker, had spent a busy year. It had been one job after another. Now that the building business had slowed a bit, he would take a rest. But where should he go?

Ostman didn't want to go someplace and just sit around. He wanted some *adventure* to go with his summer rest. He had read several stories about an old gold mine in the Canadian province of British Columbia. Many people had searched for the mine, but no one was able to find it. Searching for a "lost" gold mine! That sounded exciting. Young Ostman had no way of knowing just how exciting an adventure this was going to be!

Toba Inlet looked like a good place to start the search for the mine. Ostman traveled north to British Columbia by steamship. He then hired an Indian guide to take him to Toba Inlet.

On the way, the guide told Ostman a story about another man's search for the lost gold mine. "One day, the man found the mine in the forest. He was never seen again. Some say a *Sasquatch* [sass-kwatch] killed him," warned the Indian guide.

This was the first time that he had ever heard of a Sasquatch, Ostman told the Indian. The Indian guide explained that Sasquatch was the Indian name for a group of very large mountain creatures. "They have hair all over their bodies, but they are not animals," said the guide. "One Indian saw one that was over eight feet tall! My uncle saw the tracks of a Sasquatch that were *two feet long!*" The Indian guide said that his people were frightened of these strange apelike creatures of the mountains and forests.

The green forests of the Pacific Northwest may be home to some strange creature.

But Ostman told his guide that he didn't believe in old folk tales. He was going to set out, all alone, to prospect for gold. He was going to live by himself in the lush Canadian forest for three weeks.

After a week of hiking and camping in Ostman's hunt for the mine, something strange happened. One morning he woke up and discovered that someone—or something—had visited his campsite while he had been asleep. Someone —or something had searched his belongings, but nothing had been taken. Ostman no longer felt alone in the deep woods.

The next night Ostman decided to sleep with his loaded rifle inside his sleeping bag. While Ostman slept, the mysterious visitor apparently returned. This time it emptied Ostman's pack and carried off packages of prunes and pancake flour.

The next morning Ostman was puzzled. What kind of creature could have been poking around his camp while he slept? He knew that porcupines would steal salt whenever they could find it. But his salt had not been taken. He knew that bears would leave a terrible mess. But his bag had been emptied very carefully. He could not figure out what the creature was. Human visitors would probably have taken his money or other valuable items.

When Ostman awakened he realized a visitor had been to his camp during the night.

After three nights of unexplained visits, Ostman decided to solve the mystery. He went to sleep, fully dressed. He had placed his shoes in the bottom of his sleeping bag. He held his loaded rifle. Ostman was determined to stay awake all night and wait for the mysterious thief.

But after a day of searching for gold, he was tired. He dozed off to sleep. When he finally awoke, he wished he hadn't. Albert Ostman found himself in the middle of a nightmare.

Something had lifted Ostman from the ground and was carrying him off! To where—or *what*—he could not guess. Was he dreaming all this? Was he still actually asleep? No! He could feel the chill of the night air on his face. He could feel his body being bumped about by whatever monster was carrying him. He must still be in his sleeping bag! He could feel it wrapped around him, the hard rifle butt against his side.

It seemed an hour had passed. Ostman could not be sure. He had thought a dozen times about crying out or trying to make a run for it. But to whom could he call—where could he run? He had his rifle with him—maybe he could

What was it that was carrying Ostman, still in his sleeping bag, through the night?

shoot his captor. Could he afford to make "it"—the creature carrying him—nervous? What if he shot and missed? Ostman felt his weight shift, and he knew they were now moving up a steep hill. Whatever was carrying him, it was now breathing harder.

When it stopped climbing, the creature put Ostman down on the ground. It was still dark and Ostman saw nothing. But he could *hear* something. The sound of muffled voices reached him—more than two, maybe three or four voices! It was about then that Albert Ostman started to believe what he hadn't dared to imagine until now. The Sasquatch! He had been kidnapped by a group of Sasquatch!

It was daylight before Ostman saw what he had dreaded to see. At first he saw only their outlines as the sky began to brighten. The creatures looked something like people—but bigger and much more hairy.

Holding his rifle, Ostman asked, "What do you want with me?" They seemed not to understand and only chattered back in some strange language. Ostman saw the creatures more clearly now. There were males and females.

"I saw the outlines of four people. There were two big ones and two little ones. They were all covered with hair. They had no clothes on. They looked like a family: a father, a mother, and two younger ones. Both the boy and the girl seemed to be more afraid of me than I was of them." The gun was of no use to him. He might shoot one, but what about the other three?

Albert Ostman, the young man who had set out on a treasure hunt for gold, found himself to be the treasure of the Sasquatch for a week. He was relieved, at first, to find out that they didn't mean him any harm. But how was he going to return to civilization? Would these strange people let him go? And how would he survive until he was let go?

For a day or two, Ostman was content to play the pet. Then he started to make the tools and utensils needed for his escape. The young Sasquatch watched him as he worked. The Sasquatch treated Ostman as if he were a family pet. He was afraid that his rifle would not be powerful enough to kill one of the Sasquatch. This scared Ostman. He knew he could not take the chance of using the rifle.

Ostman decided to use his tobacco on the older male Sasquatch. One day, he started to chew his tobacco. He held out the bag to the male Sasquatch, who swallowed a great deal of the tobacco. The Sasquatch howled in pain. "The creature's eyes rolled over in his head. He looked straight up. He stuck his head between his legs and rolled forward a few times away from me. Then he squealed like a pig."

Ostman feared that the creature would come after him. But he was wrong! The hairy creature

The Sasquatch howled in pain as the tobacco burned his mouth.

headed for the water. He wanted to put out the "fire" in his mouth.

Ostman quickly picked up his gear and ran! The female Sasquatch came after him. Ostman pulled out his rifle and shot a bullet over her head. She became frightened and ran back to safety.

Ostman, having seen a chance for freedom, took it! He hurried through the forest the rest of that day and part of the next. Then he heard someone call out, "Timber!" He knew that he had found civilization.

When he met the loggers, Ostman was exhausted and feeling very sick. But he was careful in what he said to them. "When I came up to the lumberjacks, I guess I was a sorry sight. I hadn't shaved since I left Toba Inlet, and I hadn't washed for days. When I came out of the bushes, they kept staring at me!"

The lumberjacks said, "You look like a wild man! Where did you come from?" Ostman simply told them he was a prospector who had lost his way while looking for a gold mine.

"I did not tell them that I had been kidnapped by the Sasquatch. If I had, they probably would have thought I was crazy!"

Ostman kept this strange story to himself for more than 30 years. He knew no one would believe it. Only when many people began talking about the Sasquatch did Ostman tell his story.

2

What Is the Sasquatch (Bigfoot)?

Who, or what, is the creature that some call by its Indian name, Sasquatch, and others call *Bigfoot?* Who, or what, are these giant, hairy creatures that roam the mountains and forests of the Pacific Northwest and British Columbia, Canada. Are they animals? Are they humans? Are they some link between the two?

Since the earliest reports from people who claim to have sighted the monster called Bigfoot, these questions and dozens of others have been asked of scientists. And there have been a few theories proposed. Perhaps the Sasquatch are a wild tribe of oversized human beings. Perhaps the Bigfoot is the *missing link* in the evolution from apes to humans. But most scientists are still asking some more important questions. Are these creatures *real*? Was Albert Ostman really kidnapped by the Sasquatch?

Hundreds of people say they've seen the Sasquatch. Many more claim to have seen the huge footprints that have caused the creatures to be named Bigfoot. Some of the prints are almost two feet long!

It seems the Indians of the Pacific Northwest have always believed in the Sasquatch. There are certain Indian legends that have been passed along for hundreds of years. Some of these legends tell of the Giant Men of Mount Shasta. Others tell of the Stickmen of the Washington Mountains. And always there are the Sasquatch in the legends of the Salish Indian tribes of British Columbia.

The Indians have respected the Sasquatch, and they have shared the forest with them. They are sure the Sasquatch do exist. But modern

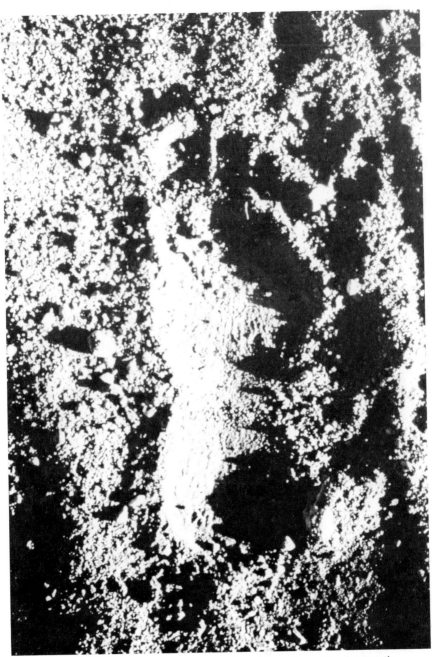

A footprint, sixteen inches long, has been found in the earth.

19

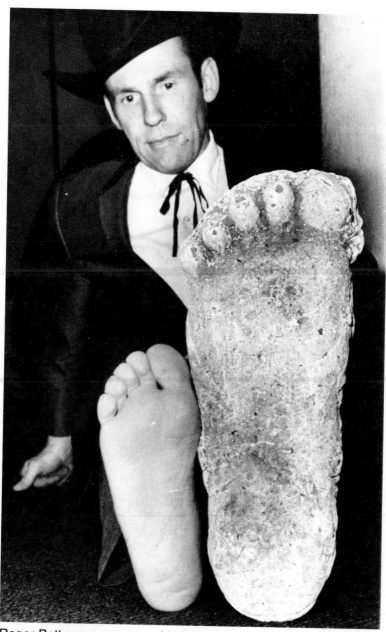

Roger Patterson compares his foot with the cast of a Bigfoot print
he made in 1967.

science has often rejected the Indian legends about the Sasquatch.

The earliest mention of a Bigfoot is in the stories of the Norsemen and their voyages to the New World from Norway. Almost 1,000 years ago, Leif Erikson and his crew of explorers found some strange creatures whom they said were "horribly ugly, hairy, and dark, with big black eyes."

In 1811 an explorer named David Thompson went to British Columbia to scout for furs. Climbing a hill in the forest one day, he came across a track in the snow that looked very strange. Thompson later reported: "I measured it. There were four large toes. Each toe had a short claw and was four inches in length. The ball of the foot was three inches deeper in the snow than the toes. The hind part of the foot did not mark well. The total track measured 14 inches in length by 8 inches in width."

Thompson was a skilled woodsman who worked for a large trading company. He ruled out any animal he had ever known. Nothing he knew could have made that footprint.

More than 70 years after Thompson explored the Northwest wilderness, workers came

Thompson found huge tracks in the snow.

to build a railroad and open the territory. In 1884 a newspaper printed a story about an adventure some railroad workers had in British Columbia. It was reported that the railroad workers had captured a strange, unknown creature they found near where the track was being laid. The railroad company had named the creature "Jacko." They planned to send him to England as a circus attraction.

The newspaper described the creature: "Jacko looks something like a gorilla. He stands 4 feet 7 inches in height and weighs 127 pounds. He has long, black, thick hair. He resembles a human being, with one exception. His entire body, excepting his hands and feet, is covered

The hairy creature was caged and fed milk and berries.

with glossy hair about one inch long. His forearm is much longer than a man's forearm and he is very strong.

"Jacko doesn't talk," the newspaper article went on to say, "but he half-barks or half-growls once in a while. He eats berries and drinks milk. His keepers refuse to give him raw meat. They fear it might make him savage."

One day, before Jacko was to have been shipped to England, another news story broke about him. The strange hairy creature had *disappeared!* Workers discovered he was gone from his cage when they brought his morning meal. Not a trace of Jacko was ever again reported.

If the story of Jacko was true at all, it was later thought the strange creature must have been a young Bigfoot. In any event, all stories of Jacko soon disappeared from the newspapers. Reports of strange creatures in British Columbia, however, did not stop. People kept claiming to see hairy creatures and finding footprints that could not be identified.

Many people supposed these reports were either false or the products of busy imaginations.

There *was* one thing about all of these stories of the Bigfoot that puzzled the people who wouldn't believe them. *All the reports seemed to describe the creature and its footprints about the same way.*

There was one story told of a Bigfoot, however, that was different from all the others. President Theodore Roosevelt once wrote a book called *The Wilderness Hunter* in which he tells the story of a hunter named Bauman.

Bauman and a friend were on a hunting trip in the forests of British Columbia. They returned to their camp one evening and found it a complete mess. Their packs had been emptied and their tents wrecked. At first the hunters thought a bear had done it. But when Bauman's friend looked at the tracks, he shocked him by saying, "That bear has been walking on two legs!"

Bears do stand on their two hind legs. But they usually don't move around that way. When they want to move, they drop down on all fours. Knowing this, the two hunters were concerned, but they couldn't think of anything to do until daylight. They decided to go to sleep.

At midnight, Bauman was awakened by a loud noise. He smelled a "strong, wild-beast odor." He looked about him when, suddenly, he spotted a large body outlined in the darkness. Bauman fired his rifle at the dark shape but missed. He heard crashing noises in the darkness as the creature rushed away into the woods.

The two hunters stayed awake until daylight. They stayed close together all day. That night they built a large, roaring fire, and they took turns standing guard. After midnight the creature came back, but it stayed at a distance. They heard the cracking of branches and a moan. By the next morning they decided to gather their traps and leave. With the sun shining, the men were not so frightened. They decided to split up. One would gather the traps, the other would pack all the gear. Bauman's partner went back to the campsite to pack.

Bauman had finished gathering the traps and walked back to the campsite. He called to his friend who was supposed to be packing. There was no answer. When Bauman reached the camp, he saw that the packs were set for travel. But he found no other sign of his friend. He checked the tents but they were empty.

About to widen his search, Bauman walked along a path about 25 feet from the camp. He found the body of his partner lying near a tree. The body was still warm. His friend's neck was broken. Four big, red marks colored the throat.

Walking from the camp, Bauman discovered huge footprints around his friend's body.

Bauman recognized the footprints around his friend's body right away. He had seen them around their camp for days. He was sure the creature who had left the prints had snapped his friend's neck.

What makes this story different from all other Sasquatch stories is that it is the only one on record of a murder by a Bigfoot. Many can't believe that a Bigfoot would kill. Others think it could be possible. But what would cause the creature to kill a human?

Is the story Bauman told Theodore Roosevelt true? Why is it the *only* report of harm at the hands of a Bigfoot? Could Bauman's friend have been killed by something other than a Bigfoot—perhaps another human being?

All About the Bigfoot

Like an ape, the Bigfoot's head is peaked, or pointed. Unlike an ape, the Bigfoot's eyes do not glow if a headlight shines into them at night.

The Bigfoot is described as having no neck and no ears. Eyewitnesses say its head seems to just sit "on top of its shoulders." Perhaps its neck and ears are hidden under the hair that covers its body.

With all the eyewitness reports of how the Bigfoot looks, moves, and acts, why wouldn't

A composite drawing of a Bigfoot based on one hundred
eyewitness reports.

more hunters have shot at them? Perhaps it is because the Bigfoot looks too human. If we can believe the descriptions people have given, the Bigfoot seems to look like a combination of ape and human being.

The Bigfoot seems to be tall, but it is not built as a tall human would be. The Bigfoot has a long body, long arms, and short legs. Even though its legs are short a Bigfoot seems to move very quickly. Witnesses say the creature never runs. It just walks very fast. And the Bigfoot is said to be a fast swimmer as well. Two fishermen say they watched a Bigfoot swim across a small lake in Idaho. They couldn't see what stroke the creature was using. Its arms were underwater all the time. But the Bigfoot did swim expertly and quickly.

What does a Bigfoot eat? According to witnesses, the creature eats plants and animals. The Bigfoot eats the same foods as many animals and humans. Experts think that the Bigfoot likes salmon and land animals. But there is one more very important clue we cannot overlook in trying to decide what a Bigfoot is—animal or human.

If Albert Ostman's story is true, the Bigfoot "family" chattered to each other. They seemed

People who have seen a Bigfoot swimming say he keeps his arms underwater all the time.

able to think and talk with each other. This sounds more human than animal. But very few other witnesses have reported hearing a Bigfoot make a sound. A few claim to have heard high-pitched screams or grunts from a Bigfoot. No one, other than Ostman, is on record as having heard a Bigfoot "speak."

A Bigfoot is said to have a terrible odor. Witnesses more than a hundred years ago told of the same odor that witnesses describe today. They say the creature's horrible odor smells like sulphur or rotten eggs. One man described it as "a wild-beast odor." Another said it was so strong

Peter Byrne, director of the Bigfoot Information Center in Oregon, at a lake in British Columbia where a Bigfoot was seen pulling up water lilies and eating them.

that he had to roll up his car window to get away from the stench. But the odor remained inside his car overnight. At the same time, there are witnesses who say a Bigfoot has no smell they can remember.

Albert Ostman claimed to have been closer than any human to a Bigfoot. Ostman never mentioned a strong odor coming from his captor.

Perhaps a Bigfoot only gives off an odor when it is frightened. The odor might be a protection, used to scare off enemies the way a skunk uses its chemical smell when it feels it is being threatened.

The only other clue we seem to have so far doesn't tell us very much more. We have the *footprints* of the Sasquatch. They are certainly different from the footprints of a human being.

The Footprints

Hundreds of people say they have seen the actual footprints of a Bigfoot or Sasquatch. Plaster casts of the footprints and pictures of those casts have been seen by millions. The footprints and the plaster casts are the proof, according to many people, that the Bigfoot does exist.

The footprints of the Sasquatch share the same characteristics. They range in size from about the size of a human foot up to 20 inches long. The entire foot rests on the ground, and

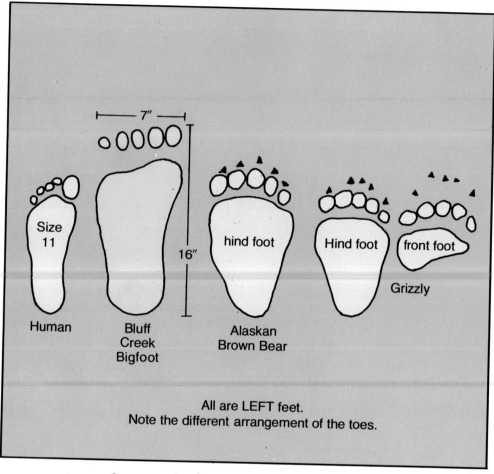

Comparison of human, Bigfoot, and bear prints.

the big toe is larger than the other toes. These are human features. But human feet have arches. The feet of the Sasquatch are flat. And the Bigfoot print is very wide. One shoe manufacturer examined a 15-inch print made by a

Sasquatch. He said that the foot would need a shoe more than 13 sizes *wider* than any shoe ever made!

A number of the footprints show only four toes. But some show five. One expert thinks the four-toed prints were made by a five-toed creature. He thinks that the Bigfoot sometimes walks with one toe off the ground.

The Sasquatch footprints are different from human footprints in one obvious way. The ball of the foot looks like it has two lumps under the big toe.

Why are there two lumps? Several different scientists have tried to explain them. A British naturalist named Ivan Sanderson looked at some print casts and decided that the creature must have very long toes with webbing between them. He thinks the lumps are thick, dead skin that protect the webbed feet from rough ground. He feels the lump is split in two so that the foot can bend.

Two members of the Academy of Sciences in Moscow, Dr. Dmitri Bayanov and Dr. Igor Bourtsev, think that the foot has two lumps because the animal's feet are more like hands. This would make a Bigfoot more like an ape than a human. An ape can hold onto a branch with its foot as well as its hand.

Mark Pettinger, Jr. holds a cast his father made of a print he thinks is from a Sasquatch.

Dr. Grover Krantz, an anthropologist at Washington State University, has studied the tracks left by 17 different Sasquatch and photographs of at least 50 others. Dr. Krantz thinks the footprints are proof of the Bigfoot's existence. He says, "Even if none of the hundreds of sightings had ever occurred, we would still be forced to conclude that a giant *bipedal* (two-legged) *primate* does indeed inhabit the forests of the Pacific Northwest."

Many scientists still feel that the Bigfoot exists only in the human mind. They will believe only what they can see and study. Whatever stories have been told, there is still no one that has caught a Sasquatch for scientific study. Why is that? The closest anyone seems to have come to catching a Bigfoot may have been to take its picture. Two people *may* have done just that—we still can't be sure.

Bigfoot Is Captured— On Film

The San Francisco Chronicle published a photograph of what may have been a Bigfoot. In the late 1950s, a weatherbeaten woodsman named Zack Hamilton brought some photographs to the newspaper's offices. He said he had been followed by a hairy creature while he was hiking in the Three Sisters Wilderness area in the state of Oregon. Mysteriously, Zack Hamilton never went back to the newspaper office. Nothing more is known about him and his photographs.

The newspaper printed one of Hamilton's photos. In the photograph, the hairy monster looked like a black blob with a head, arms, and legs. The photograph was too blurred to identify much more.

The best "photograph of a Bigfoot" was taken in 1967. Rodeo rider Roger Patterson and a friend had set out to hunt a Bigfoot in Bluff Creek in California. The two had been interested in the Bigfoot after reading several magazine articles on the creatures. They would hunt the Bigfoot, not with guns, but with a camera. It was October 20th. Around lunchtime Patterson and his friend, Bob Gimlin, rode their horses around a huge log pile that was blocking their path. The pile also blocked their view of whatever was ahead.

As they rode around the logs, they say they saw a large Bigfoot squatting on the bank of the river. As soon as the Bigfoot saw (heard?) the two men on horses, it stood up and walked quickly away.

The two men had been hoping to find one of these creatures. But they were shocked and a bit frightened to actually find a Bigfoot out in the open like that. The horses were more than shocked. They panicked!

As the Bigfoot stood up the horses panicked.

The pack horse that was carrying the camping gear ran away. Gimlin slipped off his horse. Patterson had more of a problem. His horse reared up and fell over on him. For a while he was trapped. His leg was caught under the heavy horse.

As the horse got up, Patterson struggled to get his camera out of the saddlebag and then took off after the Sasquatch. Patterson aimed his lens, pressed the trigger, and shot the film until all 28 feet were used up. The Bigfoot was gone. The excitement was over. But with any luck at all Patterson still had the Bigfoot—in his camera.

The Patterson film shows a large, dark creature walking on two legs. It has a very heavy build and is covered with hair. The focus is not sharp enough to show any details of its face, although its head can be seen. The face does not have a jaw that sticks out like an ape's. But the eyebrows do look apelike—they are ridges.

The creature has a peak at the back of its head. No neck and no ears can be seen. It has big buttocks, something apes do not have. The creature's legs and arms are thick and wide, but

Roger Patterson took this picture in Oregon in 1967. He said it was a female Bigfoot.

they don't show any muscles. When the creature walks, its feet fall heel first.

It is difficult to estimate the size of this creature. Experts who looked at the film have tried. The track of the Bigfoot measured 14½ inches. Its stride measured about 42 inches. From these measurements, scientists believe that the Bigfoot stood about seven feet tall.

But is the film real? John Green, a writer himself and a Sasquatch hunter, took the Patterson film to a film laboratory to be examined. He knew that the film industry could create almost anything with special effects.

The technical people at the film laboratory reported that the Patterson film is an original. Nobody could have fooled with it. The film is genuine.

Even if the film is real, is the Bigfoot shown in it real? Or is the creature in the film a mechanical monster? Or is it a human being in a costume?

John Green doesn't think so. One of the big problems with the "fur suit" explanation, he says, is that the shoulders of the Bigfoot are so very much farther apart than the shoulders of a large human. When the Bigfoot moves, you can't see padding. The arms swing too easily.

No one who has seen the film has been able to find a zipper. And many have looked for the "zipper" on that "fur suit." No one has been able to find evidence of any kind of costume.

What is the Bigfoot or Sasquatch? Is it a man, a monkey, or a myth? Too many people for too many years have reported seeing the same thing for the Bigfoot to be a mere coincidence

From a distance, a Bigfoot closely resembles a gorilla pictured above).

Man, Monkey, or Myth?

6

It would be exciting to have a live Bigfoot to study, if only to solve the mystery of whether or not it exists. Questions about its intelligence might be answered too.

But what would captivity do to the Sasquatch? What did it do to poor Jacko those many years ago? Captivity might kill the valuable creatures.

Of course, there are people who say that the *only* way to really prove the Sasquatch exists is to kill one. Then no one would be able to dismiss them as imaginary. "We need a piece of the body," say the hunters.

47

But most people think that killing a Sasquatch would be brutal. In the state of Washington, Bigfoot protectors have the law on their side. In 1969 Skamania County passed a law that anyone who killed a Bigfoot would be fined $10,000.

Killing a Sasquatch is not a smart idea. It's too big a chance to take. "What if we only kill one," said one small child, "and it was the only one left?"

Destroying something to prove it exists doesn't make any sense. The Bigfoot searchers should go on looking for this rare breed. Someday all the answers may be known about the Bigfoot. Today the creature remains an unsolved mystery.